Re-Enchanted

Poems for the Imagination
& Inspiration

ROB JONES

Re-Enchanted

ROB JONES

ISBN: 979-8-9856708-6-8

Tuscany Bay Books
Fruita Colorado
Star Idaho

www.tuscanybaybooks.com

This book is dedicated to the memory of my father, Robert Lee Jones. Thank you for showing me how to live fearlessly and for your constant love.

ACKNOWLEDGMENTS

First, I would like to thank my Lord for birthing these poems and making this book possible.

Thanks to my lovely wife, Genetta Jones. You are my muse, my joy, and my reason to love.

Thank you, Mary Elizabeth Jackson, for your unconditional support and friendship. Grace Scholl, thank you for blessing me with your editing skills.

Thank you, Stephen Gambill, for allowing me to use your breathtaking picture for the cover of my book. I love you, brother.

Special thanks to Jim Christina for bringing my dream into a reality. I am truly grateful for all that you have done.

I also would like to thank my family and friends for your love and support.

RE-ENCHANTED

TABLE OF CONTENTS

Enchanted &
Inspirational Poems

This poem was inspired by reading C.S. Lewis's account of experiencing an intense desire and longing for a beauty that could never truly be attained in this world.

THE SWEETEST LONGING

My heart's ensnared by a beauty that's wooing,
Lassoed with longings of silver truths pursuing.
A deep ache is conceived now that truth and story converge—
My spirit can barely bear it, to give birth to this mythic urge!
An elusive desire swept over me like a gentle autumn breeze,
Then vanished like lightning—now I'm undisguised, on my knees.
Oh, how I yearn to lay unclad beneath my numinous lover,
Clothed in agape's embrace,
where aesthetic mysteries are uncovered…
My soul pangs and bleeds from earthly stabs of joy.
Ethereal yearnings are hindered. Prayers of solace, I now deploy.
Glimpses of an inner reality—refractions from a poet's tongue—
Flush out hidden truths in this life and the life to come.
My heart is now re-enchanted by heaven's beautiful haunting;
The bitter taste of a restless craving has become my sweetest longing!

While I was contemplating how strangely beautiful God is and how I wanted to reflect that strange beauty, this piece formed and then broke the surface. By learning from Him, and mimicking Him, in all that I do, I know I will not yearn for something I may never have.

ACHE FOR A LOVER

Teach me to put dark emotions under the light
Teach me to hide illicit desires that flirt with me in the night
Teach me to bleed with the heart of the anguished,
So love may take notice, and grace may be lavished
Love, please take heed of a naked soul
That once reflected your image, and in grace was clothed
Teach me to be wild for your enchanting embrace
To hunger and thirst for your numinous taste
Oh, how I ache for a lover like you
Seduce me under a crowd of angels that weep
Tonight, man and Divinity will become complete
Devour me in your death so that I may become alive
How disturbing this must be to the soul that does not abide
If only they knew, everyone would ache
for a lover like you.

This piece was written to encourage those who are going through a difficult and a bitter providence in their lives.

JUST TO KNOW YOU

No matter what I'm going through,
You are always there for me—
To get me through the misery.

Every ounce of hope, I'll find it in you.
I'll place my life in your hands.
In your grace, is where I will stand.

At times, it seems I'm alone in this life,
But I know it's not that way;
I will trust you each and every day.

To breathe in life is to embrace your death—
I will praise you with all my heart,
For I know we will never part.

Just to know you, just to have you in my life,
I'll relinquish all I possess:
It's all in you, I must confess.

Just to know you, is all that matters in my life—
This is all that I'm living for.
I breathe just to know you more.

This is a metaphor for those who had humble beginnings and went unnoticed by people. But in spite of this, they are aware of the value, the significance, and the beauty that resides inside them.

SEED

I am just a seed—this I must admit,
But one day I'll show you, I'm much more than this.
You see this corruptible shell, and label me *pitiful;*
But inside, there's a magic that will make your world beautiful.
I am being transformed by an enchanted secret—
Rooted in a high garden where decay can never reach it.
In darkness I am hidden, disguised and unspoken,
But dawn will reveal a new life when my body's broken.
In the sun, my beauty is kindled—burning to break through;
The rain dilates the ground, which births out something new:
Wonder is now exposed, blossoming in all its glory.
My labor has bodied forth a mythological story.
Now, I'm no longer a seed—this you must admit;
In my beauty, there is meaning: reach out and apprehend it!

I wrote this poem with a longing to be more like my creator.

ESSENCE

Position me in your secret place,
Preserve my soul in your gentle grace—
Lord, I want to be the essence of true holiness.

Bring me into your sovereign arms,
Let my soul feed on your heavenly charms,
For I want to feel the essence of true holiness.

Fill me up with an endless love,
Endow me with Thy Spirit from above,
For I want to be cloaked with the essence of true holiness.

Lord, touch my hands to hold someone in prayer,
Let me be that someone who truly cares,
For I want the world to embrace the essence of true holiness.

When we encounter and surrender to something beautiful,
whether it be music, art, poetry, a story, or a piece of music,
we become enchanted by it and profoundly changed
by it when we allow it to do its job properly.
That's the idea behind this poem.

PIERCED BY BEAUTY

Pierced by beauty, now I'm no longer the same.
It left me naked, laid open, but I'm not ashamed.
Unraveled in its presence, it aids my myopic vision:
Logic and Reason are horses that transport Meaning to its mission.
Pierced by beauty, now I'm open to enchanted worlds;
Encountering deeper realities, where obscure mysteries are unfurled...
Satisfied are unearthed longings. I'm reshaped by scarred hands,
Privy to an insight—pointing beyond atoms and molecules that dance.

Pierced by beauty, now I've become awakened to wonder.
Feeding on the fruit of myth has appeased an authentic hunger.
Stealthy, Meaning has been suffused through the common,
Illuminating a charm that's hidden in a secret garden...
Pierced by beauty, now I see the world as it really is:
Charged with hallowed echoes from a king that lives.
Evergreen leaves tremble from angels passing in flight—
Piercing hearts with beauty, arousing the dead to life.

The original meaning for the word poem means to make or create, and since God created us, we are His poems, and He created us to create. So, in a sense, we are all poets.

THE POET MAKER

There's a marvelous mystery suspended in the air,
It's the tongue of the poet that makes us aware.
Incarnated wonder, robed in imagination—
In the aesthetics of language, nothing compares.
It aids the world with the gift of revelation,
And provides hope to a heart of despair.
A fountain of purpose pours through a poet's pen:
An ordinary vehicle taking us places we've never been,
Where a deeper magic is exposed-the unveiling of mysteries.
A crown of flames perched on a poet's head;
Echoing the truth with the language of fairies,
To lead us through the dark, and arouse the dead.
Let a metaphor escort you to a truth that will affect
And awaken you to a dream that you won't soon forget:
That we're all little words on the lips of the divine poet;
Undone, but serviceable poems, we're written to interject
A spell to break an unseen disenchantment…

This is a poet's glory; to usher in wonderment!
A piece about someone who wants to change but doesn't' have the
fortitude or capability to do it on their own, so they ask for assistance.

REFASHIONED

Allow me to drink in your celestial light,
To illuminate this heart which only beats in the night;
This ominous thirst has never been quenched,
So I feed on my folly, and continue my descent...
Must I be nurtured like a common beast,
And travel through the wide gate on sin's short leash?

This heavy, thick veil is my constant perception;
Commandeered by a spell of the strongest deception.
A willful prisoner in a foul dimension,
I'm settled and comfortable in Adam's malevolent affliction.
I'm like an unimpressive tree where birds do not perch;
With no purpose, no virtue—Has heaven called off its search?

Underneath, my nature is as dark as a cave.
A slither of light is needed for truth to invade.
Over and over, I've bitten this illicit fruit:
It's so beautiful on the stem, but disfigured at the root.
My palate must be cleansed—this I confess—
So I'll nurse on Emmanuel's veins, and feed on his flesh...

Holiness is being fostered, advancing deep within;
Sinful layers discarded like a snake shedding its skin.
Now, I'm cloaked in love—pulsating with new life.

Lifted by the weight of glory, my soul now takes flight...
I am now spiritually fit to respire in eternity.
It is by His scarred hands that I'm refashioned perfectly.

This poem is about a person who feels hollow and empty inside but
desperately wants to feel alive.

EFFIGY

Life-like but lifeless, a dichotomy of illusions…
Am I only observing and never participating?
Inside, I am cold as death—but burning for Hades.
An artificial soul, imbued with a delusion,
Sadly comfortable in my slavery of confusion.
Fossilized underneath a concept that's decaying—
Could I be a broken image, not worth saving?
While I have no tongue to pray for a heavenly intrusion,
You, the iconoclast, break this stony heart:
Recarve your bust, and replace this broken image,
Chip away the decay, until there's not a flaw nor mark;
Let the heat of your light burn away each blemish,
Until I become your finest work of art;
Then sing the words, "It is good," when you're finished.

There are things in this life that try to stifle and quench your imagination. This piece is meant to ignite the imagination and reveal to the reader that there is a reality beyond our perception.

BREATHE

Am I an upright amphibian, breathing in two worlds?
Inhaling enchanted air, while choking on a serpent's lie?
After death, are there no more golden apples to satisfy?
Rumor has it, when times rolls up, a garden unfurls
Where we will be re-enchanted into little boys and girls...
But in this twilight, imagination begins to retreat
And fall back into a tomb that's devoid of meaning.
Threats from the dead, at me are now hurled;
Disenchanted I've become, underneath an imprisoned sky.
With one breath, I apprehend a glimmer in the dark;
With another, I let out a derelict's cry,
Hoping heaven will ignite a truth with a mythic spark.
When I expel Adam's air and take one last sigh,
I know I'll breathe again in a country on high.

I wrote this poem on a day that my behavior wasn't in concert with my beliefs.

BROKEN

Approached by a distinguished metaphor
That pleaded for my attention,
The consistent burden of incongruity
Was the state of my disposition…

Weighed down with a destructive stature,
Now my very being is breached.
They credit me by my code of ethics,
And judge me by the lack of apathy in my speech.

Oh, Beloved, change my water into wine,
So that I may encounter your elation
And taste the rhythm of the great divine,
To embrace your death for my salvation!

But oh, this pattern of pain
Has caressed me so well…
A broken spirit is all that remains,
Now that this crippled beggar has fell.

This is a poem about self-sabotage.

PLIGHT

Shattered from a fall, by my own demise,
Gathering pieces of my soul under clouded skies;
One by one, I discard fragments in the night,
Leaving a trail of decay from a twisted carrion—
A vacant corpse that's not worth burying.
This is me, perfectly executing my plight.
I bleed in the twilight, on my knees, with guilty hands.
My soul is hemorrhaging, fading in the shadowlands…
This heart has atrophied, incapable of doing right.
I hear celestial voices echoing through my vacant soul,
Trying to lead me to the high mountain,
But their path has grown cold.
This is me, flawlessly, executing my plight.
My stature is anomalous: bent from all the weight,
And burdened by distorted gods whom I cannot placate.
I'm ensnared by my vices, which hide in plain sight,
And are marketed as freedom—but I'm tethered like a slave
And left hollowed out from the barren joy they gave.
This is me, impeccably, executing my plight.
Am I worth salvaging when the sun sets?
Or will I become my own worst regret?
Will I ever experience your power and might?
For all I ever do is feast on despair!
I guess I'm profoundly damaged, beyond repair…
This is me, immaculately, executing my plight.
Oh, Jewish Carpenter, refurbish this run-down interior;
From my very first breath, I have been inferior,
And I'm deeply wounded from the battles
I've had to fight.

ROB JONES

Faint prayers are crawling through my parched tongue—
Hoping they will reach heaven before the day is done.
This is me, no longer executing my plight.
Now everything I have, to the sovereign, I'll surrender.
Passively, I've witnessed the resurrection of my stature:
The exchange of dark garments to be cloaked in your light.
I've been pursued by eternity, Love is now my captor;
I'm harnessed in my love's embrace, for now and forever after.
This is me, redeemed from executing my plight.

I wrote this poem for my beautiful wife.

I WOULD

I would love you in ways you've never dreamed or known,
I would love you in ways no man has ever shown;
I would fulfill your innermost desires with a fervent prayer,
With a touch that's soft as a whisper, and light as air.
I would awaken feelings that you never thought existed,
That would set aflame a love wherein fire and desire are elicited.
I would get you drunk in an ocean of unbridled ecstasy,
That would have you swimming deep in love's glory.
I would take you to a place more beautiful than the stars above—
I would do this for the one who has never been loved.

This poem was inspired after I heard a lecture from the founder of The Cultivating Project, Lancia Smith.

THE GLOAMING

A dark autumn breeze, summoning my soul
Under a violet-shadowed, bruised sky.
No longer do the glowing embers console
When you're bordered by nocturnal cries…
Refractions from an old sun whose strength is fading,
Night is now inking its way forth.
My state of being is slowly decaying—
A gradual decline is taking its course.
Not entirely dead, nor am I truly living:
I'm just a beast clawing under a crescent moon,
In need of a magic moment to guide me
Out of this obscurity that looms…
Though I'm cloaked under a shadow of self-loathing,
A whisper of light will re-enchant me out of the Gloaming.

I wrote this while in the hospital room where my father was. Witnessing him in his condition was one of the most difficult days I had ever experienced.

IT HUMBLES US ALL

This is not the normal way to embrace mortality:
Probed, strapped, sedated, into a self-induced reality.
A mass of confusion, suppressing his once constant peace,
And draining every ounce of his worth and dignity...
They feed his veins with dark spells of transient relief.
Aimless, he flounders, in the murky waters of deceit.
Is there a realm in heaven that takes his soul to keep?
This person he's become has hijacked his identity,
Contradicted his behavior, and sullied his morality.
He told on-lookers: "What you see is not reality;
What you are encountering is an allegory,
A hidden meaning revealed in vulgar grief."
Now loved ones clasp palms, and quiver on bended knee;
For this is the normal way to embrace mortality.

I wrote this while feeling I was in a spiritual battle, a battle that I was losing.

OPEN SEASON

Providence has decided for me to be the hunted.
Hell has opened its assault, now I am food for the glutton.
Bombarded by seduction, unaware of the battle—
They try to slaughter me like unsuspecting cattle.
In a garden of sweet nectar, juices dripping on the ground,
I must watch my step, so I don't slip and fall down...
Prayer must be my cloak, to camouflage my weakness;
So on bended knees, I ask to be strengthened with meekness.
It's open season on my soul: spiritual practitioners are in place.
Lord, rescue your servant—deliver me by your grace!

Lord, rescue your servant—deliver me by your grace.
It's open season on my soul: spiritual practitioners are in place.
On bended knees, I ask to be strengthened with meekness;
Prayer must be my cloak, to camouflage my weakness.
I must watch my step, so I don't slip and fall down
In a garden of sweet nectar, juices dripping on the ground...
They try to slaughter me like unsuspecting cattle—
Bombarded by seduction, unaware of the battle.
Hell has opened its assault, now I am food for the glutton.
Providence has decided for me to be the hunted.

This Is the feeling I birth after contemplating how beautifully intoxicating poetry can be.

POETRY

All beauty is compared to you,
Through all epochs and ages;

Motions of words, romanticized and true,
That crowned men who were courageous.

Intercourse between rhythm and rhyme
Conceives a metaphor with meaning

That incarnates the grand sublime,
And awakens the dreamer who's dreaming…

A tongue becomes light of foot
As it dances with eloquence and pleasure.

Flowing verses leap off the book,
Providing me with sounds to treasure.

Decorating with language and sound,
Fashioning a portrait beyond wonder…

Overwhelming tears fall to the ground,
As I'm moved by the spell that I'm under.

You take me into other worlds

That reveal deep heaven's symmetry.

You are more prized than pearls—
That's why I love you, poetry.

This poem was inspired by the great poet, Malcolm Guite.

PIPE DREAM

I sit here with my pipe,
And together we dream…
I inhale and blow out magic,
Now my world is serene.
The smoke summons the muse,
Now he initiates the craft;
Creative thoughts begin to swirl—
Vivid words, I now draft.

I sit here with my pipe,
And together we share a dream…
Twenty-six letters form a poem
Inside of my smoke rings.
I light the earth with fire
In the chamber where secrets lie;
Imagination is now ignited,
When the vapors come alive.

I sit here with my pipe,
And together we weave a dream…
Expressions become corporeal,
Giving meaning to everything.
I breathe in the world
Through this vessel of my delight—
This is what I call heaven,
Dreaming while smoking my pipe.

This poem is for those who feel that they have let God down so many times that they are not worthy to be called a child of God. But if you have placed your faith in the person and work of Jesus alone, it is He who makes you worthy to be called a child of God.

STATISTIC

Creeping in is the stench of the guile,
Infecting me like a drug; my nature is now vile…

I'm pursued by debauchery—may my scent grow cold;
Now, I'm a pursuer of a vice I shouldn't hold.

I'm tending a garden planted by another;
Hidden seeds laid bare, exposed, uncovered.

My soul has been hijacked: it's unrecognizable, and barren,
Due to the neglect of being nurtured by the uncaring.

Paralyzed by a freedom that should have been resisted—
Heaven breathe into me, before I become another statistic…

This is a poem about struggling with temptation.

THE ARROGANCE OF INIQUITY

Lately, compromise has been lurking in my soul;
Perhaps, just this once, I'll perform this episode…
Dissipation has entered this careless heart,
Invited in to play the lead part.

An eternal lesson, this I must learn;
The flesh may be cool as ice,
But it's the soul that will burn.

Behold, I was fashioned in iniquity,
And in sin did my mother conceive me;
The sting of death has left its mark,
Therefore, I must nurse this wounded heart.

With a peculiar passion, I lobby for death;
How can I live righteously, when sin's in each breath?
But thanks be to God, for in Him my soul is strong—
So now, this robe of flesh can hold on.

Oft times one doesn't know when one has or is going astray. This piece is about falling into temptation and starting to enjoy it, so much so that you get caught up in it and see that the only way out of it is God's grace.

THE OFFSPRING

Grace is the offspring of love,
That brings forth a harvest of happiness:
To hold you during falling leaves,
And to find you in your darkest hour.
But now, I'm so far away from grace,
And where I am remains to be seen…
I've fallen for the seductive charm
of this broken world,
And the banquet it has prepared leaves me wanting;
Its menu is disguised with pleasures,
but they're fleeting.
Who am I fooling? I've feasted on the food
of the fallen,
And its seductive flavor has nurtured my soul.
Now this house is a host for original sin,
And has brought me into this hellish realm…
Grace, oh Grace, where art thou?
Please call your master, for I am in need of thee!

This work came about while dwelling on the concept of the origin and the
complexity of love.

LOVE

Is it only an action that takes away the gray?
If so, what is my reaction to the life that He gave?
Makes me want to cry, makes me want to try, to understand love.
Love is more than an action that tends to the fragile wound,
For it is the eternal attraction that took Him to the tomb…
Makes me want to cry, makes me want to try, to understand love.
I bleed for mercy, while sin shatters me into several pieces.
With a nervous smile, my behavior becomes more egregious.
So I pray to be clothed in a heavenly robe,
And to restore the flame of love in a heart that's grown cold.
No longer will I cry, no longer will I have to try, to understand love.

The following musing is about finding yourself, your purpose, and ultimately, becoming acquainted with the giver of your life. On this journey of self-discovery, there will be mistakes accompanied by wise decisions that will be teachable moments that will assist you on this journey and perhaps will help you discover yourself and your purpose.

SEVEN

Seven different lives, a man encounters in this space and time;
The first one is given, the rest he continues to find.
Every moment provides a window for private tears:
Some are filled with joy, some are filled to the brink with fears...
Mistakes and pain assist him on his task,
Leaving a trail of wounds that leads back to his past.
To move forward, he must let go of his ways,
And allow a vertical prayer to secure him on that great day.
Seven different lives a man encounters; for each he must account,
And obtain favor from the giver of each,
before the seventh one runs out

I wrote this while reflecting on how I used to live. And how I was compared to the man I am today.

CAPTIVE BY MY NATURE

Don't bring me good news;
I don't have the appetite for it,
For I'm held captive by my nature.

A celebration of a compromised soul
Has contributed to a state of prodigal gestures,
For I'm held captive by my nature.

Exchanging the purpose for pleasure:
I've tasted the pleasant vomit again and again,
For I'm held captive by my nature.

Flesh versus spirit: the outcome remains to be seen…
This age-old battle, I'll place in your
bloodstained hands,
For I'm held captive by my nature.

No mortal can abolish my plight;
I'm sentenced to this spoiled behavior,
For I'm held captive by my nature.

This poem exposes my spiritual clumsiness.

THE WRITING IS ON THE WALL

The freedom to be humble:
This is my strength when I am weak.
Over and over, I stumble;
Chaperoned by mistakes, escorted by defeat.

I immerse myself in the waters of grace—
I'm holding on without reaching;
Hoping that sin will vanish without a trace,
And I may come to grips with what life is teaching.

My emotions were like those of a small child;
A father of discipline, I was not.
Who could blame me for what I did?
Everything I desired, I got.

Now the fork is in the road,
The writing is on the wall;
With the past, my future has been told.
My only hope is for you to answer my call.

Allowing my mind to create while at a soulless job that massaged the egos of their employees but couldn't care less about them as people.

THEY

They try to find significance in an insignificant place.
They try to place first in this loser's race.
They inflame their pride within earshot of insincere praise—
They are left hollowed out and empty, at the end of the day.
They try to find substance in their appearance alone.
They wander around mindless, like orphans without a home.
They deposit their faith in flesh, which leaves them in want;
They will never find peace, only broken dreams that haunt…
They invest their lives in meaningless, material gain;
They will one day realize that in the end, it's all in vain.

This poem is about humanity seeing each other through the eyes of grace.
By doing this, we can truly accept, understand, and love one another.

ANYTHING

Can I hold you in my heart, ever so tenderly?
Can we make a new start, and dream a new dream?
Can we share the gift of love, the way it's supposed to be?
For you, there's nothing I wouldn't do— for you, I'd do anything.

The strength of love will break the chains of pain.
There is always a ray of hope after the fallen rain.
It's a promise we've seen: all colors in harmony…
To make this happen, I would do anything.

If only we could learn from each other,
That love blooms when we embrace all colors.
When I see you, I see the other half of me;
Without each other, we are so incomplete.

There once was a king whose throne was in God's heart;
He said he had a dream—Did his death wake us up?
In order for us to abandon selfish pride,
We must taste the tears of the one who was crucified…

This poem is for those who are tired of pretending to be someone they are not and are now searching to find themselves.

WILL THE REAL ME PLEASE STAND UP?

Don't know why, but I'm feeling rather blue;
Is it because of these unrecognizable emotions.
...Or is it only when I try to become someone new?

Fragments of me are shared while I try to find myself;
The task is profoundly concerning,
When you live to please everyone else.

No matter how hard I try, inside, I still get cut.
Now, I am vulnerable and exposed,
Emotionally naked...Have I revealed too much?

Inside, my soul is as empty as a cup;
I'm a shadow of a shadow of myself.
Heaven is asking: Will the real me please stand up?

I wrote this poem for the love of my life.

GENETTA

G is for your gentle *touch,* that's softer than a whisper;
E is for your <u>*encouragement,*</u> when my heart begins to blister…
N is for your <u>*nakedness,*</u> that clothes me in the night;
E is for the eternal *love* that embraces my soul so tight.
T is for your <u>tender</u> *kiss,* that makes my heart blush;
T is for our <u>*time together,*</u> when the world is in a rush… and
A is to let you know that I will <u>*always love you!*</u>

Being in a marriage with the one you love is the most passionate and romantic adventure that there is.

LOADED

The chambers are fully-loaded, and ready to pull the trigger;
The plan has now unfolded, with the unveiling of her figure...
She shoots with her hips—a weapon of mass destruction,
Now I'm devastated by her lips—under the spell of her seduction.
An eternal covenant confirmed by the blood that's hot like fire;
Now I'm forever fully-loaded, for my only true desire.

This was written as I was daydreaming about my beloved.

HER

An undeserved treasure that I was granted—
From head to toe, she spells *romantic...*

She's a masterpiece: poetry in slow motion.
Her fragrance charms me like a magic potion.

Genius is an understatement of her tasteful appearance:
A timeless hourglass—every moment, an experience.

For her, I would seize the stars and give the moon;
I would stop the world, and make her favorite flowers bloom.

I get lost in her words when they escape her tongue;
Now that I've found her, my life's just begun.

Words of love come easily when I think about my wife.

SUNSHINE

A precious dream has now come true,
Since the moment when I first met you.
Gazing into your angel eyes…
Just to behold you, is the ultimate prize.
Aching tears enter my heart,
The very moment we have to part.
A priceless treasure I've received:
An angel of heaven has been gifted to me.
Now, I'm overtaken by your beauty—
I try to stay calm, but you put me in a frenzy!
Selfishly, I prayed that you would be mine;
My life is so much brighter since I found my sunshine.

When I behold my wife, I become speechless.

SPEECHLESS BEAUTY

My heart is now at your feet,
Faithful like a dog to its master.
Needless to say, your beauty is elite;
There's no one like you, now or hereafter.
Guilty are the fairest stars—
For your appearance, they can't emulate.
History has told us of wars
Caused by a speechless beauty that devastates.

It's been said that "He who finds a wife finds a good thing and obtains favor with the LORD." I know this to be true.

A GIFT FROM ABOVE

Oh, how blessed and fortunate am I,
To be born at this moment in time,
To behold someone as sacred as you:
My heart is experiencing something new.

You were chosen to display the essence of true beauty;
Now, I have a notion of how ravishing angels must be.
A splendid specimen of heavenly art
That can make the weak strong, and a heart of stone fall apart.

This eternal bliss I now possess, was conceived by your smile.
Specific and private emotions will now go on trial.
My future is clear, but not yet in view—
I would rewrite history to spend forever with you.

This work just sprung up one night while reflecting on how God had orchestrated and wrote this love story that I live in.

NOT BY ACCIDENT

I find myself swept off my feet,
And now I know there's a God,
For you have become my destiny.
Your light has guided me out of the fog.

Bravely, I cried out for you,
Dying to embrace your sacred love;
I've never beheld a love so true—
Now you're all I'm thinking of.

You have pierced this fragile heart
With pleasure beyond compare.
I become moved with a million tears
When our emotions are laid bare.

Surely, it's not by accident
That we slipped and fell in love…
I know that you are heaven-sent,
My ravishing angel from above!

Surely, it's not by accident
That true love has found us here;
My purpose in life is plain to see
Because your love is near.

I wrote this after listening to a lecture by Angelina Stanford about fairy tales on *The Literary Life Podcast*. I also wanted to write a poem and call it fairy Blood.

FAIRY BLOOD

A sense of wonderment has been smuggled into my veins,
Luring me into a land that hosts deeper truths
Where my imagination invokes, informs, inflames,
A yearning that seeks union with the sacred muse…
In this enchanted realm, the veil is pulled back;
Now I'm gifted with eyes to see the unseen,
And privy to the transcendent virtues that I lack.
An arresting strangeness has awakened me from a dream.
I'm encountering a perilous journey wherein lessons are learned.
Assisted by the North Wind, I'm renovated from within;
In the heart of reality, I am now submerged;
A magical beauty forever imprinted on my skin…
I have been exposed and now conquered by the Dawn of Love,
All because I have been baptized in fairy blood.

I wanted to vent my frustration on what is going on in our country.

FEEL THE RAGE

I can't deny the thought of you heats me;
I cannot lie, you get under my skin.
I realize you try to emasculate me;
In the games you play, no one wins.

You rape the law and leave our culture desecrated.
I stand in awe and watch our demise…
It's time to do what's right before morality's desolated,
And beauty's defamed before our eyes.

You blame the place where you comfortably live,
For the reactions that others give;
The freedom that you breathe and taste—
You throw it in the Defender's face!

No longer will you run this country into the ground,
And cancel the words of the brave;
No longer will you tear this country down,
For now, it's time to feel the rage.

I wrote this while thinking about the purpose and the role of the government.

DADDY WELFARE

Once a month, your presence is felt,
Playing the role of someone else.
The concept of *free* has made us a slave,
Dependent upon the sweat that another man gave.
Shackled to dependency, chained to complacency—
Who can call himself a man, who forfeits his responsibility?
Another month approaching, the cupboard is bare;
Mommy walks out the door to receive from Daddy Welfare…

This poem is about the repercussions of injustice, but it's also how to respond and overcome injustice appropriately.

IF ONLY

If only opportunity had hovered over me like a cloud of grace,
Perhaps this dry soul wouldn't be soaked
with the rage of a thousand slaves.
If only courage would have counseled me
when I was naked and debased,
Perhaps I wouldn't be clothed with the garments
of hopelessness and shame.
If only my mind weren't shackled with cries
that have lingered for four hundred years,
Perhaps I could have faced the child in her womb, and face my fears.
If only there weren't a rope responsible for choking
the voice of a distinguished race,
Perhaps this same rope wouldn't have had to visit
the offspring of the culprit of disgrace.
If only we could stop chasing after excuses like we truly need them,
Perhaps we could reach within, and purchase forgiveness
that leads to freedom....

This poem is about asking for help to die to yourself so that you can live for a higher purpose beyond you.

AT THIS TIME

My heart is at its strongest when it's broken,
smashed, and abandoned by pride.
My faith comes alive when silence has spoken,
and the voice of fear has died...
But before I reach serenity, before I reach out and touch my fate,
I must forfeit the world around me—before it is too late.
Paralyzed by the wreckage; there's nothing left to find.
I will roll the dice and face heaven,
as you look upon me with merciful eyes.
At this time, I'm scared of every step that may lead to my despair...
Mount me on your golden wings and lift me up like a prayer.

I wrote this poem to express my love for my God.

LIFE

I can't believe the things you've brought me through;
It's plain to see that I must depend on you.
You're my everything, a heavenly dream come true—
My heart and soul are committed to your truth.

I can't deny, you made my life complete.
I rely on you to be what you called me to be.
Tears of joy I cry, for your love conquers me;
A love so deep has me drowning in ecstasy.

Come baptize me, so I'll be buried in your love;
And elevate my mind toward the things above.
When I grow weak, you become my clutch—
I'll wrestle all night, just to feel your touch.

You came like a thief and stole my heart…
Truth be known, it was yours from the start.
All that was wrong, you came and made it right;
In you I now live, because in you there is life.

This is the Gospel in the form of a poem.

BEADS OF BLOOD

One Sunday afternoon, I heard an angel crying for me.
My heart began to swell with much fear,
For I knew he saw my destiny.
I fell to my knees, and prayed away his tears...
Suddenly, I experienced something that was grand:
A heavy veil was torn from within,
And I was bought by a man with expensive hands.
Because of His death, I now can live again.
My destination changed, the moment I was freed;
I chanted simple words filled with simple truths,
Now heaven sees me as an indigenous breed.
For all eternity, I was hounded and pursued…
Thanks to a kiss that exposed His love,
I am now saved by His beads of blood.

No matter how many mistakes you make, no matter how many times you fall, love is always there to pick you up and forgive you.

SPINELESS

Easily am I bruised, for I extended hospitality to a careless kiss—
knowingly, I might add.
Flattery was her stock in trade. It seemed as though I had violated a
promise from within. I had somehow betrayed
some vital information…
If only I hadn't demanded my own way, this hickey would not be on
my soul. But rumor has it, there's a remedy for such an affliction: one
that would unmark me from my guilt and shame. Or, perhaps it would
only add another layer of sorrow to a false hope…
Perish the thought; For I will pursue this thing called love, and
become one with it. But, Oh, I am spineless when it comes to love, and
I must not be indulgent in its advances: It seems as though it has a life
of its own! This thing called love hovers over me like a sovereign
country, with all the power to destroy; and at the same time, it's like a
mother nurturing her young…
I am constantly haunted by this entity of captivating brilliance, whose
sympathetic domain may nurse this intangible bruise. Is this paranoia,
or heightened awareness? If only this crippled dreamer would
awaken…

This poem is about experiencing the pain of failure but not allowing it to overwhelm you to the point of despair.

CONDITION OF MY HEART

Imagine, if you would, a wounded stallion
Before his hour of perfection:
This is now the condition of my heart.
Is there a true logic to these lonely tears?
Will someone please explain these unwanted fears?
Rejection may be the final stroke
That resurrects the fibers of my being.
Reality to a dreamer is his dreams,
Which he tastes in that sacred moment of silence,
Wherein mysteries and secrets converge.
I need to surrender to someone—someone of an alien nature,
So that my soul may hear the sweet sounds of freedom...
Heaven, look inside me, so you may see that I'm in need of love!

We all have moments that we wish we could take back; these are my
thoughts about thinking what could have been.

MOMENT

All it takes is just one moment to shatter a lifetime.
All it takes is just one moment to lose everything I thought was mine.

All it takes is just one moment to wound the one you hold so dear.
All it takes is just one moment to leave you empty and full of fear.

All it takes is just one moment to snuff out the life you built.
All it takes is just one moment to fill you with a lifetime of guilt.

All it takes is just one moment that abandons you with empty hands.
All it takes is just one moment, to wish that moment never began…

The message of the Gospel is not trying to be good. It's about relying on the one who is all good.

TRYING

Trying to nail this behavior
Like a picture frame to a wall.
Dying to resemble my Savior,
But I've become indigenous to the Fall.

Crying with the strength of a newborn,
For I know I am helpless and frail;
Lying on the ground, spiritually deformed,
With a silhouette worthy of hell.

Relying on an alien grace—
He will be my divine enabler;
Abiding in the King's embrace,
Now I'm clothed in His sacred labor.

Engaging in too much comfort, access, and pleasure can be the biggest
obstacles in spiritual warfare.

OPEN SEASON

Providence has decided for me to be hunted
Hell has opened its assault; now I am food for the glutton

Bombarded by seduction, unaware of the battle
They try to slaughter me like unsuspecting cattle

A garden of sweet nectar, its juices dripping on the ground
I must watch my every step, so I don't slip and fall down

Prayer must be the cloak to camouflage my weakness
On bended knees I ask to be strengthened with meekness

It's open season on my soul, spiritual practitioners are in place
Lord rescue your servant, deliver me by your grace

There are so many things in this life that can veil your imagination and wonderment and hi-jack your purpose if you allow it.

THE OPTIMIST

A fallen star has landed on my conscience,
Trying to awaken me from this clumsy stupor.
But I'm comfortable in this state of indifference;
For it takes more than a cosmic occurrence
To bring this twilight mind to life.
What happened to this misguided optimist,
Who used to dream while awake?
How can he recapture that self-imposed purpose,
That animated every inch of his soul?
Maybe he could hitch a ride on a fallen star,
That would direct him back into his original orbit...
But fallen are those stars; and so, too, shall be his outcome..

This was written for those who need just a little peace and tranquility when they encounter darkness and chaos in their lives.

SLITHER OF LIGHT

Darkness, darkness, darkness, prowling proud and vain.
Pressure, pressure, pressure, tightening the reins.
Danger, danger, danger, spewing venom all around—
Running, running, running, from calamity touching down…
Mayday! Mayday! Mayday! Clouds of judgment now descend—
Allies, allies, allies, where are you to defend?
Glorious, glorious, glorious, is the king clothed in all his might.
Lord, Lord, Lord, conquer the shadows with a slither of light!

I am living proof that wishes do come true.

MY WISH

Feels as though I am alive,
Since you came into my life.
Feels as though I am complete,
Since you gave your heart to me.

Feels as though the earth stood still,
And made this moment oh-so real.
Now, I hear the angels weep,
Since you gave your love to me.

Your flowered kiss, your tenderness,
Has me all wrapped up in bliss;
I will rope the moon, make it snow in June,
Move heaven and earth, just to touch you.

I always wanted to hold you so tight.
I always wanted to love you with all my might.
I always wanted to taste your tender kiss—
Thank you for granting me my wish.

This was written for those who have loved and lost.

WHAT COULD HAVE BEEN

I'll never know what it feels like
To hold you softly under the moon,
To taste your tender kiss,
Or to dance to your sultry tune;

I'll never know what it sounds like
To hear the words, *I love you,*
To hear you breathe in ecstasy,
Or hear the echo of a love sonnet that's true…

You are so close to me, but so far.
In my lonely sky, you are my only star.
I'd risk it all to be with you,
But you are a dream that won't come true.

I'll close my eyes and turn away,
Knowing that there won't be a day,
When I don't think about what could have been;
To have that moment of being more than friends…

Now, I dread for that day to come,
When that someone will step right in
And play the part that was written for me—
And to take away my "what could have been."

A poem of a love that's unrequited.

IF YOU LOVED ME

Can't you see, I am nothing without you?
There's no more me if you should leave my life.
If I set you free, you'll take a part of me with you;
So if you won't come back, I'll just face the facts and die…

Hopelessly, my heart is devoted to your smile.
It's no longer mine—it obeys only *your* pleas.
So I'll never be free; even if I moved a million miles,
A trail of tears would lead me back to misery.

I see the sun rise because I've been up all night.
I'd packed up my tears when I awoke from this dream.
My world's not the same because you're not in my life;
You made me believe that I was your everything.

But if you loved me, it was worth all the pain:
Your devastating touch made me feel so alive.
And if I never, ever fall this way again,
Then at least I have loved in my life.

This poem is for those who had a complicated relationship.

CHANCE

If, by chance, we should cross paths again,
Maybe my shy heart won't have to pretend.
And if, by chance, I could hold you again,
Maybe we could be more than just friends.

If, by chance, I could unring this bell,
But your arms were there to catch my heart when it fell…
If, by chance, I could breathe you in again,
And dance away the night listening to Janis Joplin…

By taking a chance, I crossed the line between love and war—
I must admit, I didn't expect for my heart to soar.
Now, it's true: I'm laced with guilt and blame;
My only friend is the burden of this pain.

If, by chance, heaven should hear my dire prayer,
And remove the shades of shame from my despair…
The moment seemed so innocent at first glance;
But now I need a remedy, so I may have a second chance.

Here is a poem about a relationship that ran its course.

IN THE RAIN

You don't love me like you used to:
I can see it in your eyes, feel it in your kiss,
When you walk right out the room.

You don't want to hurt me, but you're going to.
How do I prepare, now that I'm aware
That your exit will be soon?

This is going to take some getting used to.
I'm drunk with this pain; Will I ever love again?
For I haven't got a clue...

I guess I didn't know how to love you.
Will my heart beat in vain, will I go insane,
After you say we're through?

But I must confess that I am prepared
For the scar you'll leave on my heart;
Yet still, I am somewhat scared
Of the moment when you will depart...

I look up and see dark clouds in a sky that's gray.
Is it too late to pray for change?
Somehow, we have lost our way,
While driving in the rain.

This piece came when I was in a cold and dark place spiritually and emotionally.

BITTER PROVIDENCE

The pain is so real I can hardly catch my breath;
So inside, I'm crying out for a gracious death.
My heart's too numb to feel, and wrecked beyond repair—
Oh Lord, please save me from this despair!

The storms of life have taken their toll;
Now, the blood I shed is from a wounded soul.
Jesus, touch me, before the sun descends;
For I'm feeling cold, and my world needs to mend.

I'll set my affection upon your endless grace.
Through the pain, I'm sure to find your lovely face.
Father, it feels like I'm drowning in the rain;
My throat is worn out from calling your name…

I'm lost and broken in this bitter providence—
I can hear angels weeping in the silence—
But I am holding on to your promises.
Sweet Spirit, comfort me, in this bitter providence.

Here is a poem for those who feel vacant and lifeless inside.

RESUSCITATE ME

There's something twisted in me—
My follies are ingrained in my soul.
Trying to eradicate this misery,
But the evidence of sin has taken its toll.

I can't escape this inclination.
My fallacious heart is chained and bound;
Now I'm longing for emancipation—
Amazing grace, oh how sweet the sound...

Well, I am tired of chasing roses:
Their sweet thorns are bleeding me dry.
I'm so scared inside, but no one knows it,
Because I'm wrapped in darkness—blinded by the light.

I am now choked up; breathe your life into my heart.
Lord, resuscitate me, resurrect me,
Help me to arise, and give me a new start;
Open the grave to set me free, and then resuscitate me!

This is a love poem for the lover of my mind, body, and soul.

RENEW

Oh Lord, equip my heart
To give birth to a seed of love.
By your Spirit, I can start
To set my mind on things above.

I clear my throat to proclaim your word,
Though my tongue is laced with sin—
Surely there is no need for concern,
For it's you that will set it free in the end.

I'm only righteous because you declare me to be:
By faith, this will pull me through.
You gave your life to redeem me,
Now I live my life through you.

Lord, I need you more than I did yesterday,
For I tremble at the task at hand;
Lord, I want to love you more in each and every way,
So please, renew this man.

In any relationship, communication and transparency are imperative for its success.

SILENCE

Could it be, you and me just don't take the time,
To see what is lingering in our hearts?
Couldn't we, shouldn't we, just lay it on the line,
So that we can have a brand new start?

Never thought, never knew, that love had a rage
That destroys like the bitter wind…
We're in need, so desperately, to turn another page,
So we can start to breathe again.

Now wondering, now pondering, what is lurking
Behind the lips of your silent words—
Why can't I, why shouldn't I, continue searching
For a problem that seems so absurd?

In the silence there's a still, small voice,
Beating through my heart, speaking to my soul;
In the silence we've made our choice…
The heat of the moment has left us numb and cold.

Here are some thoughts about the beautiful and strange power of the Eucharist.

RECOGNIZE

Is it true that I am this weak?
So devoid of anything good?
The horizon looks so bleak—
Divine assistance, help me if you would.

I thought that through my efforts, I could bring
A holy work that would draw you near...
I guess I'm oblivious to these things.
So, lift the veil, that I may see clear.

Summon your kingdom to live within me,
So, that I may no longer be blind.
Let grace and mercy give me eyes to see
That there's a reality outside of time.

Bread of life, I long to feed on thee,
So that we may become as one.
Wine of life, I long to drink from thee,
So that I may recognize God's only son.

This poem is about giving my life back to the one who gave it to me.

THIS LIFE

I really need to get there.
I really need to give it a go—
You must assist me because I'm helpless.
I really need to lay it bare.
I really need to let it all go.
You must dress me as the angels dress.

I really hope you pursue me.
I really hope you enter my life.
Dig all around me and plant your grace.
I really need you to blind me;
I really need to see the light.
Breathe out your word, upon my face.

I'm going to lay this sphere down,
And pick up heavenly things:
This will surely set me free.
I watch these tears fall to the ground.
Up above, I hear angels sing—
I can feel your wonder baptizing me.

I'm going to give—I'm going to give it all.
Please help me to answer your call,
So that I may surrender this life.
I want to get—I want to get it right;
I want to try—I want to try this time,
To make something out of this life.

Confessional proof that I am a beggar in need of grace.

A BEGGAR'S PRAYER

I'm tired of drifting in this blue,
I'll Cling to the rock that holds the truth;
I'm tired of breathing black and white—
Illuminate my world with your light.

I feel like the calm before the storm;
I'm dilated, so that faith can be born.
I'm seeing things I've never seen before—
The veil, from my eyes, has been torn...

Crippled and broken, here I stand.
My hope is in a man with expensive hands.
Too deaf and dumb to understand,
I put my faith in the one they call the Lamb.

Descend your ear to hear my sinful tongue:
Please come near, so we can be as one.
Is this soul of mine beyond repair?
Heaven, please answer a beggar's prayer!

The effects of original sin.

WAKE ME

There is nothing I can do, nothing I can say;
I'm helpless in every moment, helpless in every way.
It feels as though my soul is six feet down;
I believe that I am buried—engrafted in the ground.

I'm hoping for the light, hoping for some grace,
I'm desperate to reflect the glow from your face…
But I can sense the silence that's all around.
There is nothing here but darkness to be found.

There's something you can give—something in your hand,
A transfusion that will bring life into this man.
I am dead, but full of pride and lust:
I am cradled and covered in Adam's dust.

Secure me with your scars, secure me with your blood—
This is all that I need; this is more than enough.
To supplant this silent guilt and this shade of shame,
Carry me from the pleasure that leads only to pain…

Could you wake me up inside, could you make me come alive?
Replace death for life, with your perfect sacrifice?
Would you breathe your life into me, open my eyes to see,
Create this heart anew, so you could love me right through?

ROB JONES

ENCHANTED PRAYERS

From the Author

I wrote these prayers to assist those who do not know how to pray or have difficulty verbalizing prayers. Prayer is a spiritual exercise that can enrich your faith, your life, and the life of your loved ones. Prayer is a tremendous blessing; it is the language of the soul that helps us communicate our deepest needs and desires to a God who is always there to listen and answer. I hope these prayers will be some assistant to you in the bitter and sweet providences in your life.

God Bless
Rob Jones

GOD'S SOVEREIGNTY

Dear Heavenly Father,

You are most wise and all knowing. Nothing can escape your gaze, nor thwart your eternal decrees. By your holy counsel, you decree and ordain all things according to your holy will and good pleasure; yet sin does not originate with you, nor do you violate the will of your subjects. Contingencies and subordinate causes are not supplanted—but on the contrary, are established by you. When you judge the earth, your creation learns righteousness; you declare the end from the beginning. Your counsel will be upright, so that your purposes may be accomplished.

Lord, I know the trials and tribulations that come into my life are for my spiritual growth and for your glory. I know that behind a dark cloud, the light of your face will burst through and I shall never be the same. I know that you know what's best for me, and that in whatever condition I may find myself, that condition is the best for me—so that I may be reformed and conformed into the image of Christ. Thank you for carving out each moment of my life, so that faith can be fortified, and I may be spiritually fit for your kingdom. In the name of Jesus, I pray. Amen.

SURRENDERING TO GOD'S WILL

Dear Heavenly Father,

I t's not within me to surrender to your will without your Holy Spirit; for I am completely helpless under the tyranny of my fallen nature, which is continuously evil and corrupt. Please, by your grace and mercy, enable me to welcome and cherish your good and perfect will for me. I pray that my will and my heart be in concert with yours, so that I may glorify and honor you with my life. Humble me so that I may concede to heaven's agenda, while abandoning mine. In your Son's name, I pray. Amen.

A PRAYER FOR A HOLY LIFE

My God and Father,

I come to you needy, broken, and crippled, asking that the Holy Spirit give me the spiritual strength to live a life worthy of the gospel; to show me insights and the true interpretation of your Holy word, so that I may apply it in my daily living. Fill this jar of clay with your anointing, so that your resurrection power may work in me, through me, and out of me, to do the good work that you have ordained for me to perform. Cultivate my heart with holy affections, that I may be a vessel of honor fit for your employment. Let my words, gestures, imagination, afflictions, and endeavors, consummate to one purpose: to give you unadulterated glory. Help me to live every moment by placing a smile in your heart, and never a sad crease in your face. Let me always ponder on and be consumed by your glory. In the name of Jesus, I pray. Amen.

TO BE CONFORMED TO CHRIST

Dear Heavenly Father,

I come to your holy throne of grace on Christ's merits, asking that you grant me holy affections and passions that will help me mimic Christ. By the power of the Holy Spirit, grant to me a will that agrees with yours. Let me commune with you moment by moment, trusting you, honoring you, and obeying you with all that is in me. Help me to be sacrificial and loving. Cause me to reflect the light from your face, and to be the salt of the earth. Grant to me, your servant, the power to forgive, to love unconditionally, and to make peace with my enemies. Support me in these endeavors. In your Son's name, I pray. Amen.

THE LORD IS MY ONLY REFUGE

Almighty God,

Thank you for your loving kindness, which is far better than life; You are my assurance, my refuge, and my fortress. I commit all that is dear to me into your grasp, for this is the safest place they can reside. Help me to trust in you, and in your holy and wise provisions for my life. I have nowhere else to go, for you are the only one who has my best interests at heart. I have no safehouse other than your perfect love. I thank you and worship you for safeguarding all that I have: my family, my friends, my health, and my well-being. In Christ's name, I pray. Amen.

A PRAYER FOR THE UNSAVED

Most Gracious God,

You are the God of all flesh and there is nothing too hard for you; all power is in your right hand. You are full of strength and majesty. Lord, I plead with you to grant repentance, the Spirit of adoption, and to send laborers to the unsaved. I pray that the power of the gospel permeate and penetrate throughout the land, and bring about a new creation: a people who would be transformed and conformed to the image of Christ; a people who would surrender and humble themselves in your sovereignty, and rejoice in your holiness and goodness. Holy Spirit, hover over Adam's fallen race, recreate them and translate them from the kingdom of darkness into the kingdom of life. We will be careful to give you all the glory and praise that is due to you. In the name of Jesus, I pray. Amen.

A PRAYER FOR COMFORT

Most Merciful God,

I come to you broken and shaken; the circumstances that I am in have left me crippled and feeling faint. I am in need of your comfort and strength. Help me to place my trust and faith in your sovereignty. Please shower me with your grace and hide me under the shadow of your wings. Help me to see the light of your loving face behind this dark and heavy cloud. I know this trial is for my growth, but ultimately for your glory:, help me not to lose sight of this. I know that I need not fear, because you are my escort through this bitter providence; you will never leave me nor forsake me. I will be all the better when the dawn of your glory bursts through. You are my fortress, my refuge, and a present help in my time of need. You are my faith and the strength of my salvation. In Christ's holy name, I pray. Amen.

ABOUT THE AUTHOR

R ob is an author, musician, and poet. He enjoys reading, working out, going to church, and getting lost in a movie. If he is not writing books and performing music, you can find him spending valuable time with his wife and family.

SOCIAL MEDIA LINKS

Facebook:

www.facebook.com/rob.jones.5056

Website:

www.robjonesbooks.com

Made in the USA
Columbia, SC
31 March 2023

536330f7-0239-4d3c-b29b-46526297674fR01